Watson's Notes

SPECTRUM +

I. KALISKY & D. KEDEM

VOLUME 1:

First Steps in BASIC

APRIL 1985

All programs in this book have been written expressly to illustrate specific teaching points. They are not warranted as being suitable for any particular application. Every care has been taken in the writing and presentation of this book but no responsibility is assumed by the author or publishers for any errors or omissions contained herein.

ISBN 0 907792 35 9

Published by:
            Glentop Publishers Ltd
            Standfast House
            Bath Place
            High Street
            Barnet
            Herts EN5 1ED
            Tel: 01-441-4130

CONTENTS

FOREWORD

This study unit and the others which follow, will show you the secrets of writing computer programs for many varied applications, such as computer graphics, video and educational games, calculations and much much more.

While working through the study units you will actively learn the programming language BASIC by using your Sinclair ZX SPECTRUM+.

The first study unit will introduce you to some elementary terms such as 'command' and 'program', and will show you the way to use them. By the end of the first unit you will have become quite skillful in operating the Spectrum+, as well as using both colour and sounds in your programs.

As to the studying method: thought and action are constantly called for from beginning to end. The Spectrum+ and the study units are there to provide you with all the answers you may require while trying to perform the various tasks, thus making you feel confident of what you are doing. As you work through the units you'll find that we've left some writing for you to do! When you come to a gap in the text like this ＿＿ just fill it in.

Just one more word of advice, always try to solve the problems by using your knowledge and resourcefulness before taking the easy way out and turning to the answers provided for the unit. Be bold! Experiment! Don't be afraid of making mistakes, that is the only way to really learn and to turn programming into an enjoyable experience.

Wishing you every success

DANI KEDEM & ITZHAK KALISKY

Chapter 1

THE COMPUTER AS A TYPEWRITER

Writing and correcting errors using the computer

☐ Write your first name here: _JOHN_

This will also be the first thing we'll ask the computer to do. How?

Really nothing is easier!

You have to tell it to: PRINT

To do this, you must press the PRINT key, which is located here:

☐ Now press the key!

What does the screen display?

(Choose the correct answer.)

A

B

C

? By the way, can you see a flashing symbol appearing on the screen ∎?

This is called the CURSOR, which shows where the computer will place the next thing you type.

To make the computer print your name you must write it between quotes like this:

```
PRINT "john"
```

? How are you going to get the quotes?

□ Press the key:

? Are there any quotes displayed on the screen?

If you held the key down for too long you will have more than one set of quotes. (If not, press it now to get 3 or 4.)

Right, what are we going to do now?

? How will you get rid of the quotes you don't need?

Simple!

□ Press the DELETE key and watch the quotes vanish!

You will find the key here:

REMEMBER!

A brief press of the delete key will always rub out the character immediately to the left of the cursor.

⌷ Now press the quotes keys again to get the quotes after 'PRINT'.

If you have done this successfully, the screen should display the following:

PRINT "

Now continue writing your first name. To do this, type in the appropriate letters, e.g.

        PRINT "catherine"

and don't forget the closing quotes!

Getting the Command into the Computer's "mind"

So far you have typed in a command telling the computer that it should print something. To get this carried out, or 'executed', by the computer you must get the message into the computer's brain, or memory.

⌷ To do this, press the **ENTER** key.

By pressing this key, the command is **entered**

into the computer's memory and the computer then carries out the command.

Where has the computer put your name after pressing the ENTER key ____ ?

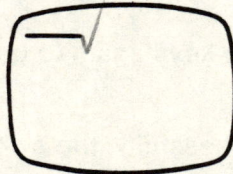 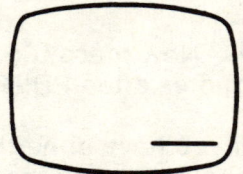

A   B

If you answered A, then you have successfully performed the various tasks.

If you have answered B, it means that there is a mistake somewhere. You may have omitted to press the ENTER key, thus not put the command into the computer's mind, or you may have forgotten to type in the closing quotes.

In this case, its probably easiest to begin again!

The Computer Message ' Ø OK '

Look at the screen.

In addition to your name, the computer has printed a message at the bottom:

Ø OK; Ø:1

(The character with a line through it 'Ø' is a zero. Zeros are always drawn with a line through them, to distinguish them from the letter O, as in Octopus.)

The above message appeared after the computer executed the command you had entered.

In the first part of the message the computer reports back ' Ø OK; ', that means the command has been successfully executed. (The second part of the message, Ø : 1, will be explained later.)

Remember, whenever a computer message does not begin with the number Ø it means that some problem has arisen in executing your command.

You will learn what the various messages mean further on.

⬜ Now tell the computer to write the letter X and repeat it some dozen times one after the other like this:

```
PRINT "XXX....XX"
```

ADVICE

To get a large number of X's you only have to keep the 'X' key pressed down.

In fact, if you keep your finger on any key long enough, it automatically repeats. The same applies for deletion as well.

Don't forget to enter the command into the computer by pressing ENTER.

⬜ Press a few keys one after another. Then erase all the characters at the bottom of the screen by continuously pressing the DELETE key.

Clearing the Screen:CLS

Before going any further, we shall tell the computer to clear the screen by using a special command: CLS (an abbreviation for CLEAR SCREEN).

The CLS key can be found here:

☐ Press the CLS key and put the command into the computer's mind (ENTER).

The computer should have cleared the screen of everything that was written on it earlier. You can do this anytime the screen becomes too full of rubbish!

Let's repeat the task of writing your name, but this time include your surname.

Insert a space between your two names like this:

```
PRINT "First name   Surname"
```

☐ To obtain this space, press the SPACE key:

☐ Now type in your surname.

Don't forget the closing quotes.

To get the computer to execute the command, press the *entry* key.

Writing in Capital Letters

You may have noticed that the computer has printed your name in **small letters**.

CAPS SHIFT

Should you wish to write something in capital letters, the **CAPS SHIFT** key must be used. There are two and you can use either.

☐ Tell the computer to print your first name and surname again (don't forget the PRINT and quotes), but this time, hold the CAPS SHIFT key down while typing in your name:

Keep your finger on one of these keys while pressing the letter keys.

A Short Exercise to Summarise this Chapter

Get the computer to print a short message using both capital and small letters.

INTERIM SUMMARY

Let's see what we have learned up to now, it's quite a lot really:

- Using the **PRINT** command.
- Typing quotes to get your name on the screen.
- Deletion of mistakes.
- Putting a command into the computer's mind - **ENTER**.
- Typing capital letters while using the **CAPS SHIFT** key.
- Clearing the screen: using the command **CLS**.
- Recognising the computer message Ø O.K.

14

Chapter 2

A SPECTRUM OF COLOURS

As implied by its name, the Spectrum+ is notable for its ability to use a wide range of colours on the screen (providing, of course, that it is plugged in to a colour T.V!).

We can start to enjoy the colours at this stage.

Choosing the Border Colour

First we shall ask the computer to colour the outer part of the screen, the **BORDER**, in **RED**.

⬜ To do this type: BORDER 2 (using the BORDER key).

The BORDER key can be found here:

You must then type 2 to get the colour red.

When you have done that, the command BORDER 2 will appear at the bottom of the screen.

⬜ Now enter the command (press the ENTER key).

You can see that the computer has coloured the outer part of the screen red.

NOW, EXPERIMENT A LITTLE!

The computer will change the colour of the border if you choose a number from Ø to 7. So try it. Press the BORDER key followed by a number and then press the ENTER key.

NOTE

You can ask the computer to colour the border in BLACK if you like.

To do this, you have to use the 'Ø' key.

☐ Try it!

What happens when you tell the computer to colour the border white?

☐ Give it a try!

❓ What is going to happen if you ask the computer to colour the outer part of the screen in colour number 8: using BORDER 8 ?

☐ Give it a try!

In this case the computer will tell you that it is an 'Invalid colour'. There is no such colour and the computer will say the same thing if you try to use larger numbers.

Let us summarise.

There are eight colours:

Ø   Black
1   Dark blue
2   Red
3   Purple (Magenta)
4   Green
5   Pale blue (Cyan)
6   Yellow
7   White

Note

On a black/white TV the various colours give decreasing shades of grey from Ø (black) to 7 (white).

COLOURING THE BACKGROUND ON WHICH THE COMPUTER PRINTS

We are about to ask the computer to write on the central area of the screen, which we will colour in each of the various colours you now know.

To do this, you have to use the **PAPER** command.

❓ What do you think would happen if we used the following command?

    PRINT PAPER 4;"abcde"

⬜ To get an answer, tell the computer to execute it.

After pressing PRINT, you have to press **PAPER**.

The **PAPER** key is located here:

The PAPER command is found on the **Key Base:**

KEY BASE AREA

KEY TOP AREA

Until now, you have only used the commands which appear on the **Key Top:**

To obtain the commands which appear on the Key Base areas you must change into **EXTEND MODE** on the computer.

⬡ To do this press the **EXTEND MODE** key:

Notice how the ▣cursor changes to an▣.

⬡ Now press the PAPER key.

Unfortunately **LPRINT** appears and the cursor changes back to▣.

DELETE the 'LPRINT' command.

❓ So how do you get the PAPER command?

Look carefully at where PAPER appears on the key. It is on the key base below LPRINT. This means that you must go into Extend mode and then hold down the **CAPS SHIFT** while pressing the **PAPER key.**

⬡ Try it now!

If no mistakes have been made, the screen should display:

     PRINT PAPER

▣
and the cursor should change back to

⬡ Next type the number 4.

⬡ Now you have to type a semicolon (;).

The appropriate key is located here:

Afterwards add "abcde"

⬜ Now ENTER that into the computer's memory.

You can see that the computer has printed the letters on a green background which is being used by the computer like a piece of paper.

⬜ Now tell the computer to write your name on yellow paper.

What colours are the spaces going to be in the following PRINT command:

    PRINT PAPER 3;"xxx   xxx"
                    ↑
                 spaces

⬜ Give it a try!

You can see that the computer prints the spaces in the same colour as the paper.

What are you going to see on the screen after you tell the computer to write on black paper (∅):

    PRINT PAPER 0;"xxxxyyyyzzzz"

⬜ Try it out!

Are you confused?

An explanation

When no special command is given, the computer prints the letters and characters in black. Therefore, when the PAPER is coloured black as well, you are unable to see anything. (A really invisible ink!)

How can you manage to see what you write on a black background?

In this case you must use another colour when writing the letters, your Spectrum+ can do this as well!

WRITING IN COLOUR

Should you wish to write in one of the colours shown in the list on page16, you must use the **INK** command. This controls the colour of the characters appearing on the TV screen, like the colour of the ink in a pen that you write with.

☐ What is the screen going to display after telling the computer:

        PRINT PAPER 0; INK 7;"123456"

☐ Try it out!

The INK command is located here on the keyboard:

INK appears on the keybase, just like the PAPER command. Therefore, you should carry out the same procedure as you did to obtain PAPER (see pages 17-18).

☐ Enter the command into the computer.

The computer is now printing in white.

☐ Now tell the computer to write a sentence, using **yellow INK** on **red PAPER**.

Well, as you see, you can tell the computer to **PRINT** messages on a coloured **PAPER** with coloured **INK**.

Let's stop here for a moment and look at the screen. You can see quite clearly that the screen is divided into two areas.

The outer part (the BORDER) and the central area (the PAPER). (If they are both set to the same colour, change the colour of one of them now.)

The computer writes in the central area!
You write on the outer part, at the bottom.
The computer messages are also displayed at
the bottom of the outer area.

This is the area where the computer writes.
Let's call it:The **Screen**.

This area is set aside for your instructions or
for the computer's messages.

From now on the central area will be referred
to as the 'SCREEN'.

Back to the Colours

If you want the computer, whenever you use
the PRINT command, to print in white INK on
green PAPER, you don't have to type PAPER 4
and INK 7 each time you enter a PRINT
command. You can set the computer up when
you start, by executing the two commands, to
make it, print using white letters (7) on green
paper (4), all the time.

To do this, the commands, may be typed one
after the other:

```
PAPER 4 : INK 7
```

Between the two commands is a colon (:), this
is used to separate two or more commands on
the same line.

The colon can be found here:

22

⊔ ENTER the two commands into the computer's memory.

The computer tells you that the two commands have been entered and executed, but still, nothing has actually happened on the screen!

? What do you expect will happen now if you tell the computer to print something?

⊔ Tell the computer to print some letters.

Now you can probably see, that it produces white letters on green paper! From now on, whenever it is told to print something, it is going to do it using white INK on green PAPER unless you decide to change one of the colours!

⊔ Tell the computer to print something else, and again it will be in white on green.

? Are you curious to know what happens if you tell the computer to clear the screen-CLS?

⊔ Enter the CLS command into the computer's memory.

You can see now that the computer clears the screen by using the green colour already stored in it, that's why we get a green screen!

? What is going to happen if the following command is entered:

   PAPER 2

⊔ Press the ENTER key and tell the computer to write something.

As you can see, the computer does write on RED paper, but using WHITE letters.

? What is going to happen should you decide to use the CLS command now?

⊔ Give it a try.

You can now play with the colours, changing the BORDER, PAPER and INK as you like.

A LITTLE EXERCISE

Tell the computer to do the following:

PRINT your name in white letters on red
PAPER (a red strip at the top of the screen).

     your name

     yellow screen

   magenta border

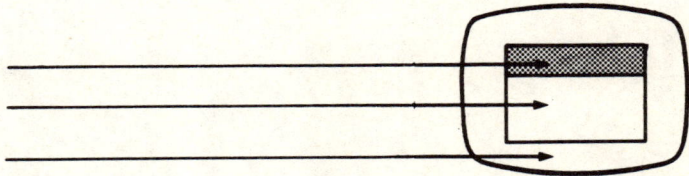

Clue: to get a yellow screen, use CLS as well.

(Answer 1).

Have you finished?

Change back to the standard colours of the
computer:

- white border

- white screen

- black ink

Do all this with a set of commands followed
by pressing the ENTER key only once!

Clue: For writing a sequence of commands
turn to page 22 or look at Answer 1 in the
Answers Chapter.

Chapter 3

THE SPECTRUM AS A POCKET CALCULATOR

Arithmetic Calculations

Your computer is not just an advanced 'colour typewriter', but an advanced calculator as well.

ADDITION

☐ Tell the computer to execute the following command:

    PRINT 2+5

(don't type any quotes this time).

The + symbol can be found here:

You can see that '+' is on the key top between LIST and K. To obtain commands and symbols located in this position on the keys you must use one of the SYMBOL SHIFT keys.

☐ Hold down the SYMBOL SHIFT and press the + key.

☐ ENTER the command.

❓ What has happened?

This time the computer has carried out the calculation and printed the correct answer. Now that you know how to operate the Spectrum+ as a pocket calculator, get it to do the following sums:

Exercises:

> 5+3
> 199+1
> 3000 + 5000

? Did you remember to use the PRINT command?

MULTIPLICATION

☐ Tell the computer to work out the answer for the following:

> 5 x 3 = ?

As 'x' means the letter 'X', the '*' is used as a multiplication sign.

It can be found here:

DIVISION

☐ Tell the computer to calculate the following:

> 20 ÷ 4 = ?

Wait!

The division sign for the computer is "/" (as in 20/4) and is found here:

SUBTRACTION

⬚ Tell the computer to deal with the following:

    21 – 7

⬚ If you are familiar with negative numbers try:

    7 – 21

The minus sign can be found here:

Now you can try some other kinds of arithmetic as well.

⬚ How about trying the following:

    20/4*6-10=?

⬚ Before going any further, clear the entire screen (**CLS**).

A RIDDLE

❓ What does the ↑ symbol stand for?

⬚ Type in the following:

    PRINT 3↑2

The ↑ symbol can be found here:

(Don't confuse it with the cursor key at the bottom of the keyboard)

What result have you got?

What will you get if you tell the computer to do the following:

2 ↑ 3

4 ↑ 2

(If you are still not clear about what is happening see Answer 2)

PRINTING A SUM BETWEEN QUOTES

What can you expect if you insert a calculation in quotes as follows:

PRINT "2+5"

Type in the sum including the quotes.

Have you got any result?

The computer has just **copied** the calculation without working out the actual answer.

Remember! Anything typed in between quotes is simply copied by the computer and displayed on the screen!

How would you tell the computer to print the sum **and** calculate the result as well?

What do you expect to get when you tell the computer:

PRINT "2+5="2+5

Type this in and press the ENTER key. The computer has refused to execute the command!

? What does it tell you?

    `PRINT "2+5="`▨`2+5` ▪

It has found a 'spelling mistake' in your command. You can probably see a flashing question mark appearing exactly where the mistake is.

The computer needs to be told when it has to finish printing things exactly as they are (i.e. between quotes) and when to start to do the calculation.

This is done by separating the two parts of the command by means of a semicolon ';'

The semicolon appears here:

The command should be:

    `PRINT "2+5=";2+5`

▢ Correct the command and ENTER it into the computer.

If the screen displays 2+5=7 then well done! The command has been successfully corrected.

LET'S SUMMARISE

When you type a command and enter it, the first thing the computer does is to check whether you have used the language properly. It makes sure no 'spelling mistakes' have been made. If a mistake is found, the computer refuses to execute the command and uses a question mark to indicate the location of the error. It is up to you to decide what correction has to be made.

☐ Now, tell the computer to display the following calculations on the screen with the correct results:

$$90 - 14 = ?$$

$$27 / 11 = ?$$

$$26 \times 29 = ?$$

AN IMPOSSIBLE MISSION

☐ First clear the screen and then tell the computer:

PRINT 1/0

which means 1 divided by zero.

❓ What does the computer tell you?

☐ It is unable to divide by 0!

"THE COMPUTER HAS MADE A MISTAKE"

Sometimes people say: "The computer has made a mistake", but in fact, it is normally the user who has made the error.

Let's see how this can happen:

PRINT "2 + 2 =" ; 2+3

☐ Enter this little exercise into the computer.

❓ What is happening? Is your computer incapable of doing arithmetic calculations?

Not at all! It is perfectly obedient and has carried out your instructions to the letter.

In this case, it has simply copied what you have typed out between quotes, and then, without doing anything with it, evaluated the sum outside the quotes, which is not the same.

Try to enter out an expression based on multiplication to 'trick' the computer.

FURTHER WAYS OF MAKING CORRECTIONS

Type in the following command, just as it is:

```
PRINT PAPER 6 INK 2"30 * 6="6
```

Press the ENTER key.

What does the computer tell you?

It has found a 'spelling mistake' in the command you have copied:

```
PRINT PAPER 6?INK 2"30*6=";30*6 L
```

What have we omitted?

Let's correct that line without deleting anything! After all we just need to add a semicolon.

How do we do this?

(Answer 3)

The L must be moved to where the semicolon should be inserted. To do this, you must operate the left facing arrow ⇦.

You will find the key here:

☐ Press it and you'll find that the question mark disappears.

Get the ⬛to where the semicolon should be inserted, i.e. where the question mark was. When the cursor has reached this point type in the semicolon.

❓ Can you guess what will happen, if you press the ENTER key.

☐ Once you've corrected the mistake, give it a try!

The computer has now found another 'spelling mistake'!

To correct it, use the right facing arrow (⇨). Get the cursor to where the correction should be inserted and add another semicolon.

When the correction is done, the cursor remains 'inside' the line. You don't have to get it to the right hand end before pressing ENTER. You can leave it where it is and just press ENTER.

Go on, try...

☐ Now type in the following command:

```
PRINT "122456789"
```

☐ Don't press ENTER yet .

There is a 'mistake' in the above number sequence. Which number should be replaced?

To correct the 'mistake' you have to delete the figure 2 (the second one) and type 3 instead. As you already know, you don't have to wipe everything out to do this.

⬭ Get the **L** cursor positioned so as to enable you to delete the extra '2' like this:

        PRINT "122 **L** 456789"

Remember, the DELETE key rubs out the character immediately to the left of the cursor!

⬭ Having deleted the extra '2', insert the number '3'.

⬭ Press the ENTER key to see whether the corrected line has been accepted.

A SUMMARISING EXERCISE

⬭ Tell the computer to work out the following expression, using the colours indicated:

        22 * 13 / 7.5 - 21 = ?

The expression should be in yellow ink on blue paper
The result should be in red ink on green paper

(Clue: Write a sequence of commands separated by semicolons.)

The decimal point can be found here:

⁇ Having problems with this?

⬭ Turn to Answer 4

SO FAR SO GOOD

In the first three chapters you have learned to use the computer as a 'colour typewriter' and a calculator. However, these are not the only reasons why it is considered so powerful a machine.

What then, are the qualities which make your computer such a useful tool?

The next chapter will tell you that!

Chapter 4

SIMPLE PROGRAMMING ...

A COMPUTER PROGRAM

☐ Enter the following command on the computer.

(Don't forget to type the number before the command.)

10 PRINT 5+7

☐ Put the command into the computer. (ENTER)

? What has happened?

If no mistakes have been made,
the screen should display:

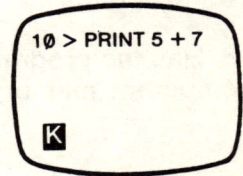

```
10 > PRINT 5 + 7

K
```

? Has the computer executed the command ____ (Yes/No)?

No, this time you have written a tiny program, a one liner, line 10

Whenever a command is preceded by a number, the computer knows that it is a program line. After pressing ENTER, the computer stores it away in its memory, where it is kept but not executed!

When will the computer start working on the program which is stored in its memory?

That is done by using the **RUN** key.

Do this now and don't forget to press ENTER as well.

The RUN key is found here:

What has happened?

It is only now that the computer has started working on the program stored in its memory, and printed out the result:

(5, 7, 12) ?

After the computer has executed the program, the line '10 PRINT 5+7' is no longer displayed on the screen.

Has the program been wiped out of the computer's memory as well?

To answer this question, press the ENTER key again.

Is the program being displayed again (yes/no)?

Conclusion:

The program has been kept in the computer's memory although it has been executed.

☐ Add the following line to the program:

    20 PRINT "Bob"

(of course, you can use your own name instead of Bob).

Store this as well in the computer's memory.

❓ How many program lines appear now on the screen_____ (1,2,3)?

If your answer was that there are two lines on the screen now, you are doing fine.

The new line, 20, does not replace the previous line, numbered 10, but is included with it.

The computer is now storing a two line program in its memory.

☐ Run the program (RUN).

❓ What line has been executed first _____ (10, 20)

☐ Tell the computer to display the program. (Press ENTER again.)

Now add another line:

    5 PRINT "Jones"

☐ Enter it into the computer.

❓ Does line 5 appear at the beginning of the program or at the end?

38

The computer stores the program smallest line number first and then the larger ones. (The order in which the lines were originally entered does not make any difference.)

⬜ Execute the program (RUN).

❓ What does your screen look like now - A, B or C?

```
┌──────────────┐      ┌──────────────┐      ┌──────────────┐
│  surname     │      │  surname     │      │  first name  │
│    12        │      │  first name  │      │     12       │
│  first name  │      │    12        │      │  surname     │
└──────────────┘      └──────────────┘      └──────────────┘
      A                     B                     C
```

If you have answered A, so far so good.

We can see that the lines are executed in the order that they appear in the program.
    First line   5
      then line   10
  and finally line 20

⬜ Tell the computer to display the program on the screen.

⬜ Now insert the line, between lines 10 and 20, that will get the computer to do the multiplication:

    5 x 40

by completing the line:

    5 * 40 ____ ____

After typing in the program line, run the program.

❓ What have you got?   A, B or C ?

```
┌──────────────┐      ┌──────────────┐      ┌──────────────┐
│  surname     │      │  surname     │      │  surname     │
│  12          │      │  12          │      │  200         │
│  first name  │      │  200         │      │  12          │
│  200         │      │  first name  │      │  first name  │
└──────────────┘      └──────────────┘      └──────────────┘
 A                     B                     C
```

If your answer is not B, then you've got a small problem:

If you didn't know, which number to give to the new line, then here's a clue:

     5.....

   1Ø.....

the new line should be inserted here

    20.....

⬜ Tell the computer to display the program on the screen (ENTER).

❓ What do you think, would happen to line 10 which is already stored in the computer if another line 1Ø, below, is entered into memory?

    1Ø PRINT 1Ø*3

When you've thought it out, try it.

⬜ Enter the line into the computer.

You've probably realised that the new line has simply replaced the previous line 1Ø At this stage, the computer remembers only the new line and the previous one has been forgotten.

⬜ RUN the program to prove it to yourself.

ADDING A LITTLE BIT OF COLOUR

⬜ Can you figure out what would happen if we added the line:

    3 INK 2

⬜ Add this line to the program already stored, RUN it and see what happens.

AN EXPLANATION

When the computer reaches line 3, it is told to use red INK. Therefore, from then on it will print out everything in red INK.

☐ Where would you have to insert another line, so that only line 5 would appear in red, and all the subsequent lines would be printed in the standard black ink?

☐ Enter the line telling the computer to do this.

(If you have any difficulties, turn to Answer 5.)

NOTE:

Now you can probably understand why the line numbers are not written in the program one after the other: 1,2,3...; but rather jump over a few numbers. For instance: 10, 20 30

This enables us to insert additional lines to improve or change the program.

Whenever you insert a new line, make sure that it is spaced a few numbers from the previous lines, to make room for more lines should they be necessary.

WIPING OUT PROGRAM LINES

Examine the first three program lines:

```
3   INK 2
5   PRINT "your surname"
8   INK 0
```

You already know that in order to print only your surname in red INK you could have written line 5 as follows:

```
5 PRINT  INK  2;"your surname"
```

☐ Enter line 5 as above, instead of the line 5 already in the program. This will only affect the INK colour for this line.

But now, lines 3 and 8 are superfluous!

☐ How can they be rubbed out? Nothing is easier!

To do this type the number of the line to be
deleted and ENTER it into memory.

For example:

⬜ To delete line 3: type 3 and then press
ENTER.

The computer replaces the existing line 3 by
an empty line 3 thus removing it from the
program.

⬜ Delete line 8 as well.

Now, on running the program, you will see that
only your surname is written in red ink!

REMOVING PROGRAMS
STORED IN MEMORY

It is now time to move on to other programs, so
the program already stored in the computer's
memory must be wiped out.

⬜ To do this, press the NEW key and then,of
course, ___ ?

Having entered the 'NEW' command, the
computer wipes out the program stored in
memory, the screen goes blank for a moment
and the 'Sinclair' copyright message appears at
the bottom of the screen.

Should you try to display the program (by
pressing ENTER), the computer would not
display anything because there's nothing
there! There's no point therefore in trying to
run the program either.

PROGRAMMING WITH THE 'GO TO' COMMAND

Examine the following program:

```
10 PRINT "your name"
20 GO TO 10
```

The GO TO command tells the computer: move to line number _10_ ?

Can you guess what the screen will display when running this program?

☐ Enter the program into the computer.

Here is the GO TO key:

Run the program

What have you got on the screen?

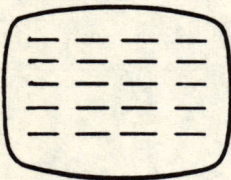

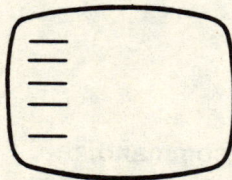

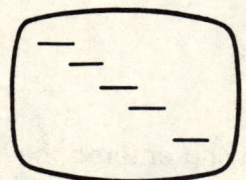

Can you now understand what line 20 does in the program?

Let's go through that step by step:

☐ The computer first executes line _1_ (10, 20) and your name appears in the top left-hand corner of the screen.

It then moves to line _____ (10, 20) where it gets to the GO TO command.

Line 20 tells the computer: GO TO line (10, 20).

As the computer is highly obedient, it executes line _____ (10, 20) again.

It writes your name once again, beneath the previous one, and then goes to line 20 again. On reaching the GO TO command it returns to line 10 yet again.

So, this program simply runs forever - or nearly!

The following arrows indicate what is going on in the computer:

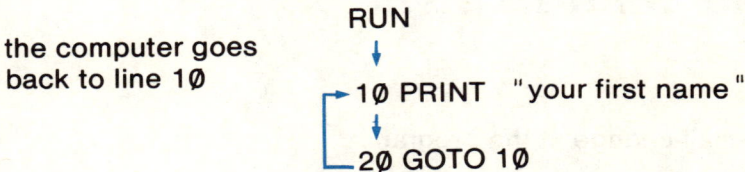

RUN

the computer goes back to line 10

10 PRINT   "your first name"

20 GOTO 10

The arrows indicate that the computer moves backward and forward between line 10 and 20 creating a sort of endless **LOOP**.

SCROLL

At the bottom of the screen you can see a message asking you whether you want the computer to execute 'SCROLL' (screen roll). It's really asking: "Do you want the display to move up on the screen, making room for new lines to be printed at the bottom of the screen?"

The program stored in the computer at the moment does not really call for SCROLL, so we won't bother now. However, we will refer back to it later, so that you can see what it is really used for.

☐ Answer the computer and tell it that you are not interested in SCROLL:

☐ Press the N key (for NO):

BREAK MESSAGE

At the bottom of the screen the computer tells you that it has stopped running the program, and excited from it - BREAK. At this stage, pressing ENTER will display the program on the screen. Give it a try!

EDITING AND CHANGING THE PROGRAM

Let's introduce a small change in the program.

☐ Add a semicolon (;) at the end of line 1Ø

    1Ø PRINT "your first name";

? How are we going to insert the change without having to rewrite the whole line?

☐ Press ENTER to display the program on the screen.

(If the program is still running and the computer asks "SCROLL?" give a negative answer by pressing 'N' and then 'ENTER').

☐ Examine the program displayed on the screen:

? In line number _2_ (1Ø, 2Ø) there is an 'arrowhead', which is called the **Program Cursor.** To insert a change in line 1Ø the cursor must be moved to it.

To get the cursor from line 20 to 10 you must press the arrow facing upwards (⬆):

If all is well, one press on the correct arrow key will move the program cursor to line 10.

Now we have to tell the computer that we are interested in making some changes in line 10, where the program cursor now appears.

To do this, you must press EDIT, thus informing the computer that we are about to make a change in the line.

You will find the EDIT key here:

Press EDIT and see what happens.

If everything is alright, line 10 drops down to the the bottom of the screen and is ready for editing.

Let's make the change now.

To add the semicolon (;) at the end of the line, you have to move the cursor to the right, to the point where the change is to be made, (in this case to the end of the line).

To do that use the right facing arrow (➡).

Have you noticed that the cursor has changed from K to L?

(Incidentally, a ▦ cursor tells you that the computer is waiting for one of the instructions that appear on the key tops, like PRINT, or for a program line number.)

⬜ Now add the semicolon (;), and then store the new line in memory (ENTER).

❓ Has the correction actually been made to line 10?

⬜ If so, RUN the program!

Which pattern have you got?

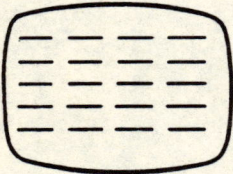

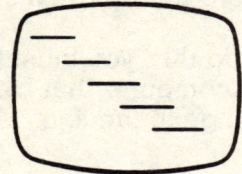

Using a bit of imagination you could think of this design as a kind of carpet. If you have not got 'carpet' C then you have a problem. Go back a few stages and try again.

Your program should look like this:

```
10 PRINT "your first name";
20 GO TO 10
```

❓ What does this program show?

It shows that a semicolon at the end of PRINT statement tells the computer to PRINT the next item **immediately** after the previous one, if there is room in the row.

When no semicolon is present each PRINT is executed at the beginning of a new row, just beneath the last PRINT.

Let's explore a little using what we have just learned. We shall change line 10 and see which 'carpet' we produce.

⬜ Change line 10 to:

```
10 PRINT " your first name ";
```

Remember:

To effect a change in line 1∅:

- Move the program cursor (arrowhead) to line 1∅, if it is not there already. ⬇⬆

- Move the line down for editing (EDIT).

- Move the cursor to the appropriate place in the line. ⇨⇦

- Insert the change.

- Get the corrected line into memory (ENTER).

- RUN the program.

CREATING A NEW LINE BY USING AN EXISTING ONE

☐ Edit line 1∅ again, so that the computer prints your name on red paper.

☐ RUN the program.

Now we wish to add another line to the program, so that your name appears alternately, once on red paper and once on yellow

red yellow red

DON'T LEAP IN YET!
There's a short cut!

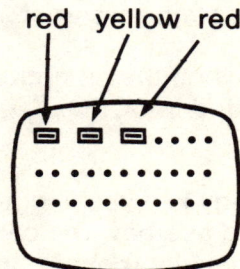

To make the writing of the new line a little bit easier, you can use line 1∅ which already forms part of the program.

How? Well, line 10 appears as follows:

```
10 PRINT PAPER 2;" your first name ";
```

To get the new line, you only have to change two numbers in the existing one. The line number changes from 10 to 12, and the colour from red (2) to yellow (6).
You can use line 10 to write line 12!

☐ Display the program on the screen and get line 10 down for editing.

☐ Now, insert the appropriate changes in the line to get line 12. (If you don't remember how this should be done, turn back to page 45.)

☐ After carrying out the required changes, put the new line into the computer's memory. (Press ____ ?).

You now have a 3 line program:

10, 12 and 20

☐ RUN the program.

☐ Add further lines with the different colours, using the same method, and each time you will get a new coloured 'carpet'.

This time, when the computer asks you if you are interested in SCROLL, give it a positive answer.

☐ Press any key you like (except for SPACE and 'N') and see how the carpet is rolled upwards to make room for another piece.

NOTE

Each time the computer asks: "SCROLL?" the program stops running.

Each time you answer "Yes" (by pressing any key except for SPACE or N) - the program starts running again.

Don't forget: when you've finished, NEW will clear the computer's memory!

TASK

⬜ Write a program which appears on the screen as follows:

Clue: play with the space before and after your name

yellow paper

green border

the name in red

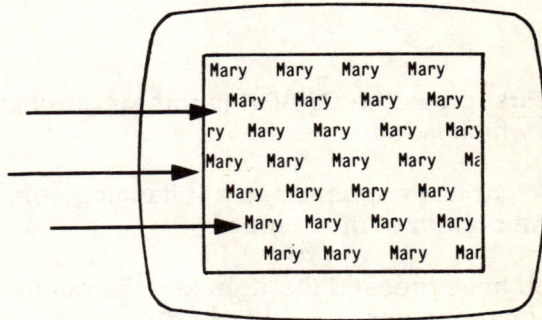

```
Mary    Mary    Mary    Mary
  Mary    Mary    Mary    Mary
ry  Mary    Mary    Mary    Mary
Mary    Mary    Mary    Mary    Ma
  Mary    Mary    Mary    Mary
Mary    Mary    Mary    Mary
  Mary    Mary    Mary    Mar
```

❓ Got it right?

⬜ Add two more program lines, like the first (1∅), but using different colours (see the previous page) and RUN the program.

⬜ Tell the computer to SCROLL the screen.

❓ Tell the computer to clear the program from memory using the command ____ ?

WALL TO WALL CARPETS

⊔ Examine the computer keyboard. On the top row of keys you will see various graphics characters:

■ ▣ ◪   and so on

Let's now use these characters in order to 'weave computer carpets'.

❓ How do you get these characters?

⊔ First press the GRAPH (short for graphics) key, which is found here:

❓ What has happened to the flashing cursor at the bottom of the screen?

If you have pressed the right key the cursor has changed into: ___ (**E**, **L**, **G**).

When the cursor displays the letter **G**, it means that you can get the graphics characters.

⊔ Now, keep your finger on the SYMBOL SHIFT and at the same time press any one of the graphics keys in the top row. Look at the screen and you will see that it displays the character that appears on the key you pressed.

Take care that you don't press the GRAPHICS key again, as this will change the **G** cursor back into **L** .

⊔ Now - press the same keys without pressing the SYMBOL SHIFT:

Do you get exactly the same graphics characters _____ (Yes/No)?

When SYMBOL SHIFT is **not** pressed, an inverse form of the graphics character is displayed.

We get black instead of white and vice versa!

For example, when pressing 2 and Symbol Shift we get:

Whereas, pressing 2 on its own produces:

To see this clearly, press the 2 key, once in combination with SYMBOL SHIFT and once without, while putting a SPACE in between.

In a short while we will use this inverse feature.

When you no longer want to draw graphics characters, press the GRAPH key again and the cursor becomes an ▉.

Now, since you already know how to get graphics characters, let's write a program which will turn the entire screen into a carpet of various graphics characters.

Have you forgotten the commands needed to write the program? If you're really stuck read on for some help, but try to do it on your own.

CLUE: You have to write almost the same program as the one which made a carpet from your name. This time, though, use graphics characters instead of your name.

Remember:

To get a graphics character in the program you must:

1. Press these keys:

2. Print the graphics characters you want

3. And finish thus

You can get out of the graphics mode just by pressing the GRAPH key a second time.

⬜ Run the program you have written.

❓ How do you like the carpet you have woven?

⬜ Now try to add to it, change the graphics characters, and see what interesting carpets you can make.

❓ Would you like an attractive carpet with your name embroidered on it?

⬜ It's really easy. Add a line to print your name between the graphics characters and run the program.

⬜ Now, as we did on page 48, add some colour commands, so that the carpet will display a large variety of colours.

A SURPRISE!

⬜ Clear the program from the computer's memory. (If you have forgotten, see page 11).

⬜ Now, type in the following program:

```
10 PRINT "▦▦  your name  ▦▦";
20 BEEP 0.1,10
30 GO TO 10
```

(don't omit ';')

BEEP   COMMA   DECIMAL POINT (.)

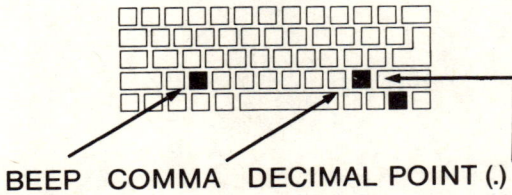

⬜ Note: BEEP appears on the key base.

If you don't remember how to get it, see page 17.

⬜ Run the program and listen!

INVESTIGATING BEEP

⬜ Change the numbers in the BEEP command and see what happens:

```
20 BEEP 0.1,10
```

Try numbers from 0 to 2.0 here.
Try numbers from +20 to -20 here.

When carrying out your experiments its best stick to the number limits given above!

TWO USEFUL TIPS

1. Don't delete a line whenever you want to change it, but edit it, whenever you can.

2. If the BEEP gets on your nerves just press the BREAK key.

CONCLUSIONS

BEEP <first number, second number>

☐ The first number in the BEEP command sets the ____ (length, pitch) of the sound.

☐ The second number in the BEEP command sets the ____ (length, pitch) of the sound.

(Answer 6)

If you know how to read music you can use BEEP to get particular notes.

For further information, see the Sinclair BASIC programming reference book.

A Summary of the Chapter

You have learned to make the screen display 'designs' of various forms and colours. You have also learned to use the computer to produce sounds of various pitches and lengths.

However, you have learned something far more important. You have learned how to write a program, store it in the computer and run it.

True, the programs you have written were quite short but, as you become more experienced, you will be able to write programs which are much more complicated, more sophisticated and really exciting.

Chapter 5

Robot Graphics

PRINT AT

Here is 'Robert' the friendly robot:

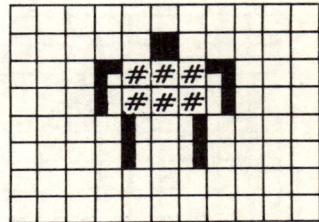

By the end of this chapter you will be able to see him on your TV screen. (In the next chapter he will even do some exercises).

You will be able to do all this by using the PRINT AT command, which tells the computer exactly where it should print things on the screen.

◻ Press the NEW key to get rid of the old program (if there is one).

◻ Now, type in the following line:

```
10 PRINT AT 2,6; "Y"
```

◻ Run the program.

? Do you understand what happened?

The PRINT AT command has two numbers after it, separated by a comma. These tell the computer which row and column to start printing at. Thus ' PRINT AT 2,6;"Y" ' tells the computer to print the letter Y, 2 rows down and 6 columns across.

The following grid divides the screen into small squares. The computer can print only one character in each square.

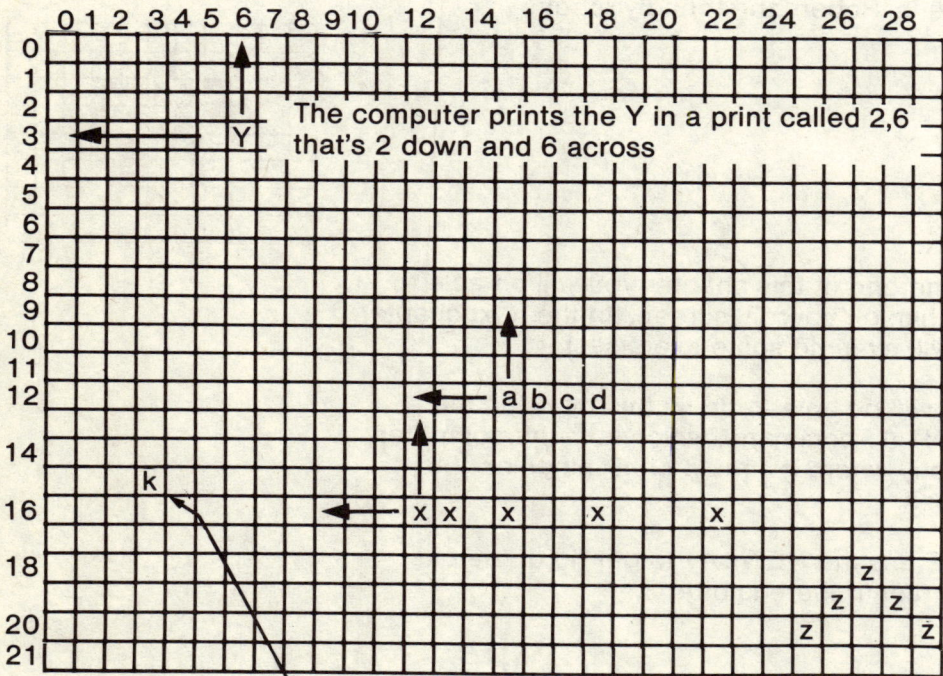

The computer prints the Y in a print called 2,6 that's 2 down and 6 across

Add a program line, which will print this 'K':

20 _____

(Answer 7)

As you can see, by using the 'PRINT AT' command you are able to print anything you like, anywhere you like on the screen.

☐ Add just one more line to print the 'a b c d' which appears on the grid above.

Clue: work out where on the screen the first letter is to be put, the computer will take care of all the rest.

(Answer 8)

Add another line which will print out the line of X's. (Pay particular attention to the spacing).

(Answer 9)

Draw the triangle of Z's on your screen.

(Clue: This time you will need 3 lines...)

(Answer 10)

What are we going to get if we change line 10 to:

    10 PRINT INK 4;AT 2,6;"Y"

When you've thought it out, change line 10 and run the program.

(Having trouble in changing the line? Turn back to page 47 for details of editing.)

TASK

Change all the program lines in the above manner, so that the screen displays the following:

- y - in green (already done)
- k - in black
- a b c d - in red
- xxxxx - in pale blue (cyan)
- All the Z's - in blue on a yellow background!

Compare what you have done with Answer 11.

Yet another task

Add further lines to the program so that each
PRINT operation is accompanied by a sound
(for instance, BEEP Ø5,12)

(Answer 12)

☐ Add just one program line that tells the
computer that after all the letters are displayed
on the screen, to wipe out just the letter Y!

(Clue: Print SPACE at the appropriate place...)

(Answer 13)

USING LIST FOR RAPID EDITING

Let's say that you would like to make a change
in line 2Ø

You want it to print 'H' instead of 'K', i.e.

```
2Ø PRINT AT 15 , 3 ; "H"
```

☐ Don't make the change yet!

☐ Press ENTER to display the entire
program. The program cursor appears at this
stage in line 8Ø since it is the last line you
wrote. To change line 2Ø the editing cursor has
to be moved to line 2Ø - quite a journey.

However, there is a simple and rapid technique
for getting the program cursor to any line you
want:

☐ Tell the computer:

```
LIST 2Ø
```

and press ENTER

Mrs Ormrod.

Mr & Mrs Preston.   Bob.

John. H. Pryce.

Mrs Reed.

Mr & Mrs Rossetto. (Aust)

Mrs V. Roberts.

Miss P. Slater.

Mr R. " last ~~Fees~~

Mr A " K to S.

Mr & Mrs Timmis (Gilbert)

Mr " & " Mr Taylor.

" " " " D Thomas. Vera ~~

Mrs. Rose Turner.

Mr & Mrs Tomlinson (Arlene)

Mr " Mrs Wogden. (Mary)

Mrs Waite.

Joe Webb

Mr " Mrs D Wilson   David

" " Walsh.   Eric.

Walter Wall.

Mr & Mrs J. Young.   (ICI)

sao

Prog 30/12

Prog

XMAS. 1 " OtO. to O28 +

S.1

⊙oo⊙ — OtO

? The computer displays the program from line 20 onwards and the **program cursor** appears in line ____ (2Ø, 8Ø).

LET's SUMMARISE

LIST makes the screen show the program lines. A number typed after the LIST command tells the computer to display the programs lines from that number onwards.

☐ Now make the change in line 2Ø so that 'K' is replaced by 'H' and RUN the program to see if you have been successful.

☐ When you've finished that, remove the entire program from the computer's memory. (NEW).

TASK

Write a 2 line program which will print the numbers 1 to 4 in the form of a square:

1 and 2 in red ink   1 2
3 and 4 in green ink 3 4

Hint: before writing the program, use a pencil to mark on the grid on page 61 the locations where you want them to appear on the screen. Then start writing the two program lines:

1Ø _____

2Ø _____

(Answer 14)

TASK

Write a 6 line program which will display the following shape at the centre of the screen:

Hint: line 1Ø –
           line 2Ø –
           line 3Ø –
           line 4Ø –
           line 5Ø –
           line 6Ø –

30

Note that lines 2Ø, 3Ø, 4Ø and 5Ø are almost identical, make use of this when writing the program. (Have you forgotten how? See page 47).

After changing into GRAPHICS mode you have to use, alternately, SHIFT to get the various graphics characters. The character ◥, for instance, is generated by pressing the number 7 key without SYMBOL SHIFT.

(Answer 15)

Now we can go back to Robert the robot.

☐ Wipe out all the previous programs.

☐ Type in a line which will print Robert's head somewhere in the centre of the screen:

1Ø ————————————————————————•

SOME ADVICE

☐ After writing each line, RUN it to see whether you are satisfied with the results.

To make it easier, use the screen grid provided below.

☐ Continue to write further program lines which will print out the entire robot:

2Ø ————————————————————————

3Ø ————————————————————————

4Ø ————————————————————————

5Ø ————————————————————————

The program only needs 5 lines!

Clue:

Remember to type spaces when drawing the legs.

The # character appears on the 3 key.

(Answer 16)

Robert will continue to appear....

Don't get rid of the program, Robert is going to do some exercises in the next chapter!

SOME PRACTICAL ADVICE

It's a good idea when you draw a robot (or any other shape) to use the grid to design the shape before writing the program.

TASKS FOR FUN

If you intend to take a break before going on to Chapter 6, here are some interesting tasks for you to undertake:

- Turn Robert into a colourful robot.

- Draw the flags of various countries.

- Create some cars and ships on the screen.

Chapter 6

Robert doing exercises

Movement on the screen (Animation)

Our friend Robert is an energetic sportsman:

Position 1: Hands down:

going back
to position 1

moving to
position 2

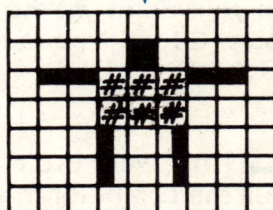

Position 2: Hands sideways :

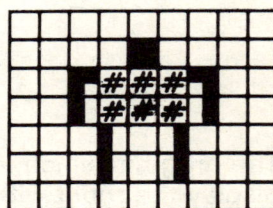

You are about to write a program which will get Robert to do some exercises.

First, though, let's consider how this program is going to be structured. Professional programmers always define the structure of their programs before writing them and so shall we.

Question

When moving from 'hands down' to 'hands sideways' should the 'hands down' be wiped out before the 'hands sideways' are printed?

64

☐ Of course! If this is not done, you would see both the 'hands down' and the 'hands sideways' on the screen at the same time.

Thus, the program will have the following structure:

The program which tells the computer to display the robot with hands down has already been stored in the computer's memory by following the instructions in the last chapter.

(If you've not got the program refer back to page 60 and type in the program to display Robert.)

☐ Now, write two more program lines, which tell the computer to wipe out JUST the hands of the robot:

60_____

70_____

Clue: Want to rub something out? Print a SPACE over it!

You may copy lines 20 and 30 and, instead of hands, print spaces!

☐ Run the program to see whether Robert's hands have actually been wiped out.

By the way, if you had any trouble removing Robert's hands without damaging his delicate body, you may resort to the following bit of programming:

PRINT " ᵒᵒᵒ "

SPACE

By doing this, the hands are wiped out by printing SPACE and the body is actually printed again.

If you are still having difficulties, turn to Answer 17.

▢ Write one more line which will tell the computer to print Robert's hands extended sideways and again, be careful not to damage his body.

80 _____

▢ Run the program and examine the results.

At this stage the robot carries out his exercises at a rather incredible speed. This problem will be overcome later. In the meantime, after you enter each line, check to see whether your instructions are being followed. Continue as planned:

▢ Wipe out 'hands sideways':

90 _____

(Copy line 80, change the line number to 90 and print SPACEs instead of hands).

▢ Add another line which will tell the computer to revert back to the lines displaying the robot with 'hands down'.

100 _____

Refer at all times to the program plan on the previous page!

☐ Run each stage to check the results on the screen.

(Answers 18)

If no mistakes have been made, Robert is now doing exercises on your television at a super-human speed. His different hand positions are almost indistinguishable.

BREAK

First, let's stop the program running:

☐ Press this key and hold it down:

Pressing the BREAK key tells the computer to stop running the program.

BREAK Message

The computer tells you: 'BREAK into program'. That is to say, it isn't running the program anymore.

It also tells you which line was being executed when you pressed, e.g. BREAK, 40:1. That means, line 40 was the last line which was executed.

The 1 stands for the number of the command in the line. Since each line may be made up of a few commands separated by colons (:), the computer lets you know exactly where it was stopped.

For instance, 60:3, means that the computer has stopped in the third command in line 60.

☐ Run the program again and again and stop it (BREAK).

❓ Does the program always stop at the same line?

IMPROVING THE PROGRAM

Let's tell Robert to slow down a bit.

When writing the program, where would you insert the commands to tell Robert to take a rest?

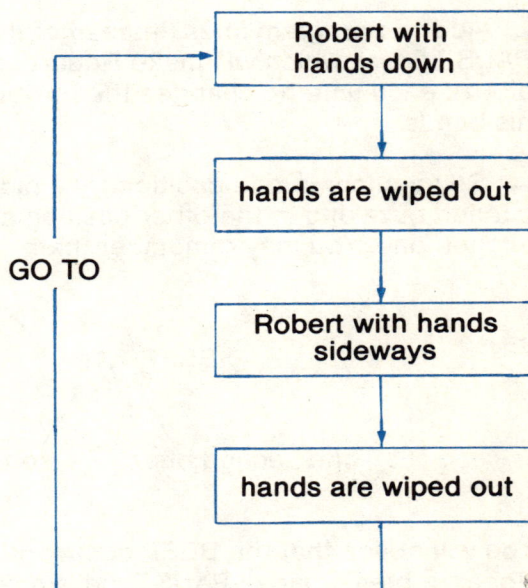

Would you insert a pause here ____ (Yes/No)?

Would you insert a pause here ____ (Yes/No)?

GO TO

Perhaps here ____ (Yes/No)?

Or here ____ (Yes/No)?

PAUSE

In order to get the computer to hang on for one second before getting on with things, just put 'PAUSE 5Ø into the program.

Insert the command PAUSE 5Ø at those points in the program which, in your opinion, call for a rest.

Be careful not to leave Robert without hands!

(Answer 19)

Want to change the pace of the exercise?

HINT:

PAUSE 25 = a break of half a second.

PAUSE 1$\emptyset\emptyset$ = ____ (1/4 second or 2 seconds?)

TASKS

☐ Add two program lines (instead of the PAUSE lines), which will make Robert produce a buzz each time he changes the position of his hands.

☐ Suggestion: In one position try a high pitched buzz and in the other position a low pitched one. You may remember that:

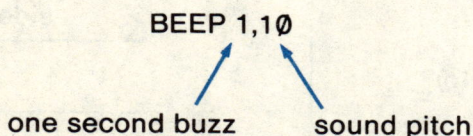

BEEP 1,1$\emptyset$

one second buzz   sound pitch

(Answer 20)

You will notice that the BEEP command gives Robert a break just as PAUSE did, since the computer does not run the rest of the program until the buzz is over.

COLOURING THE ROBOT

You can make the robot change colours while performing the exercises, and so on. Here are some suggestions:

Blue head

green sleeves

red shoes

yellow body on cyan background

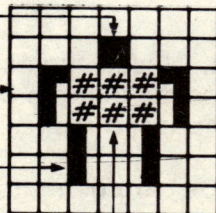

Another Exercise

Write a program, all by yourself, to make the
robot move from 'hands down' to 'jump
position'.

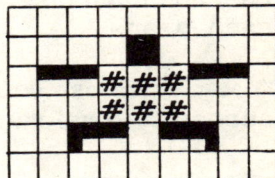

A FINAL CHALLENGE

Tell the computer to print the following face so
that:

- Its eyes will move.

- Its tongue will flick.

- It will change colours.

- It will buzz and waggle it ears.

- It will do whatever you tell it to.

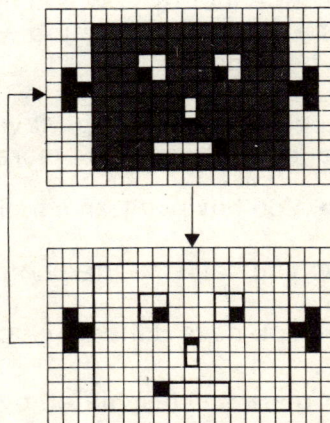

REVIEW INDEX

The following is a list of terms which you have learned in this study unit.

Examine each one of them and see whether you can remember what each means.

(You can refresh your memory by referring to the page numbers appearing in brackets next to each item).

(7) PRINT	(20) INK	(50) SYMBOL SHIFT
(8) CURSOR	(21) colon	(53) BEEP
(8) quotes	(25) PRINT 2+5	(55) PRINT AT
(12) CAPS SHIFT	(28) 4↑2	(58) LIST
(8) DELETE	(28) PRINT "2+5"	(66) BREAK
(9) ENTER	(36) RUN	
(11) CLS	(41) NEW	Computer messages:
(12) SPACE	(42) GO TO	(10) Ø OK
(12) Capital letters	(43) SCROLL	(66) BREAK
(15) BORDER	(44) Editing arrow	
(17) PAPER	(50) GRAPH	

CONCLUSION

You have now come to the end of the first study unit.

We hope that by now you have got the hang of programming and feel that you can handle a job which may have seemed rather difficult at the beginning.

You have learned to print various designs and robots but, you have also learned are much more.

● You have written simple programs.

● You have inserted corrections and improved the programs.

● You have done some calculations with the Spectrum.

If you are still fascinated by this whole business..

Get started now on Unit 2.

Details about the subsequent units are mentioned at the end of the book.

ANSWERS

Answer 1:

    BORDER 3: PAPER 6: CLS : PRINT PAPER 2;

    INK 7;"⬜⬜⬜⬜⬜⬜ your name ⬜⬜⬜⬜⬜⬜ "

NOTE: CLS turns the entire screen yellow! (PAPER 6)

Answer 2:

The symbol ↑ signifies 'to the power of' in computer language.

Thus 2↑3= 2 x 2 x 2 = 8

i.e. two to the power of three is the same as multiply two by itself three times.

Similarly 4↑2 = 4 x 4 = 16

Answer 3:

We have forgotten the semicolon (;).

Answer 4:

    PRINT PAPER 1; INK 6;"22*13/7.5-21="; PAPER 4;

    INK 2;22*13/7.5-21

Answer 5:

The additional line is:

    8 INK Ø

Answer 6:

                    BEEP 1,1Ø

length of sound   sound pitch
(in seconds)

Answer 7

```
80 PRINT AT 15,3;"K"
```

Answer 8:

```
30 PRINT AT 12,15;"a b c d"
```

Note: You only need to tell the computer where to put the first character (a). The Spectrum+ positions the rest for you.

Answer 9:

```
40 PRINT AT 16,12;"xx☐x☐☐x☐☐☐x"
```

(☐stands for SPACE)

Answer 10:

```
50 PRINT AT 18,27;"z"
60 PRINT AT 19,26;"z☐z"
70 PRINT AT 20,25;"z☐☐☐z"
```

Answer 11:

```
30 PRINT INK 2;AT 12,15;"a b c d"
40 PRINT INK 5;AT 16,12;"xx☐x☐☐x☐☐☐x"
50 PRINT PAPER 6; INK 6;AT 18,27;"z"
60 PRINT PAPER 6; INK 6;AT 19,26;"z☐z"
70 PRINT PAPER 6; INK 6;AT 20,25;"z☐☐☐z"
```

Note: The 'K' in line 20 should not be coloured since it appears in black anyway.

Answer 12:

The following lines are added:

```
15 BEEP 0.5,12
25 BEEP 0.5,14
35 BEEP 0.5,16
45 BEEP 0.5,18
75 BEEP 0.5,20
```

25

Answer 13:

```
80 PRINT AT 2,6;"☐"
```

Answer 14:

A possible answer would be:

```
10 PRINT INK 2;AT 2,4;"1 ☐☐☐☐ 2"
20 PRINT INK 4;AT 7,4;"3 ☐☐☐☐ 4"
```

You can, of course, print the square on the screen anywhere you like.

Answer 15:

```
10 PRINT AT 14,22;"▛▀▀▀▀▜"    "    see the
square on
20 PRINT AT 15,22;"█ ☐☐☐☐ █"   "    the next
page
30 PRINT AT 16,22;"█ ☐☐☐☐ █"   "    Yours is
probably
40 PRINT AT 17,22;"█ ☐☐☐☐ █"   "    displayed
somewhere
50 PRINT AT 18,22;"█ ☐☐☐☐ █"   "    else, but
this is
60 PRINT AT 19,22;"▙▄▄▄▄▟"    "    not too
important.
```

Answer 16:

```
10 PRINT" AT "8,15;"▰ "       Don't worry
if your
20 PRINT AT 9,13;"▛∘∘∘▜" program as
different
30 PRINT AT 10,13;"▰∘∘∘▰"
coordinates, its the shape
40 PRINT AT 11,14;"▰☐▰"       that
counts.
50 PRINT AT 12,14;"▰☐▰"
```

Answer 17:

```
6Ø PRINT AT 9, 13;"⬜°°°⬜ "
7Ø PRINT AT 1Ø, 13;"⬜°°°⬜ "
```

Answer 18:

```
8Ø PRINT AT 9, 12;"▬▬°°°▬▬ "
9Ø PRINT AT 9, 12;"⬜⬜°ọ°⬜⬜ "
1ØØ GO TO 1Ø
```

Answer 19:

```
55 PAUSE 5Ø
85 PAUSE 5Ø
```

Answer 20:

```
55 BEEP 1,7
85 BEEP 1,12
```

Comment:

The screen is divided into:

22 rows (from Ø to 21)
and
32 columns (from Ø to 31)

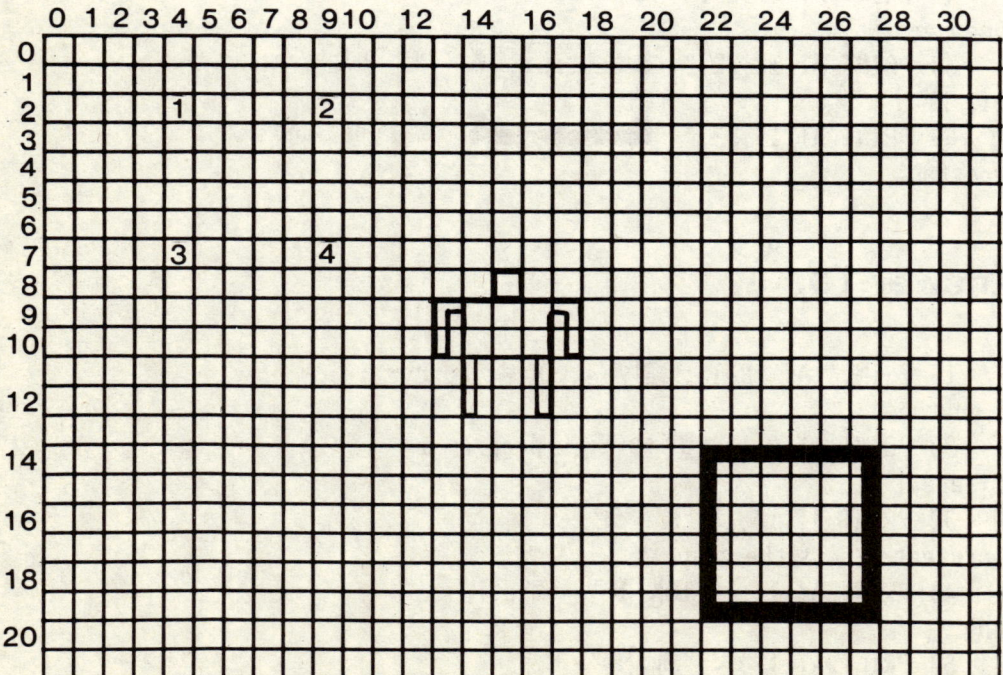

NOTES